A Look Into A Twenty-Something's Notes App

Kaylee Holsten

BookLeaf Publishing

India | USA | UK

A Look Into A Twenty-Something's Notes
App © 2024 Kaylee Holsten

Presentation by *BookLeaf Publishing*

Web: www.bookleafpub.com

E-mail: info@bookleafpub.com

ISBN: 9789363315716

First edition 2024

To all who wonder if they're alone. You are not.

ACKNOWLEDGEMENT

I would like to thank my parents for all their love and support and my closest friends Miriam and Maggie for navigating through life with me all these years.

PREFACE

These poems were written at different times in my early twenties. An ungodly amount of my poetry comes from a place of sadness but I have done my best to balance out the sad with the hopeful to better illustrate what it's like to be twenty in the 2020's.

Time To Get Up

Life is too short to always be on time

With the heaviness of presence

With the ebb and flow of mine

Stop to smell the roses

Or just the shirt you wore the day before

And get out into the wild world

That calls like waves to the shore

Wild

Thoughts are getting blurry
Like the flavors on my tongue
Nights are getting heavy
As we stay forever young
When the vodka tastes like water
And the music just won't die
We'll dance until our clothes fall off
Or until the bar runs dry

Chug

My courage drains out of my eyes at a drip.

I try to catch it in a red Solo cup.

And I tell myself I'll drink it all back down one
day.

But at this party, full of everyone's red Solo
cups, I think mine has gone missing.

Every last bit of liquid courage

Drained to the last drop.

Counting Calories

It's a pain to always be fat.
I'll just say it.
And when the skinny girl asks me
Why it's always on my mind
What I really want to say is
"Are you fucking blind?"
But I don't.
As I swallow my rage
I mark it down on my calorie chart.

Later

Sitting on my bed
Thinking of all the things I should do
But I don't want to get up
Or have to tell you
So I'll lay here in my bed
Tangled uncomfortably in the covers
Because getting up would remind me
Of this impending dread that hovers

Sleep Siren

The pillows were just so-

Soft

The blankets invited me in

The warm embrace of my dreams-

Welcomed me like an old friend

A Pest

Dry wind for words on a deserted night.

I laid in my bed.

And I cried-

A pile of sand blown away on the breeze,

Made by Time and it's Lovers-

A temporary flea.

Rumple Stiltskin

I have this thing

Where I really have nothing

And I spin it all up till it turns into something

But I spin too much

Straw turned gold back to straw

And in the end I have nothing

But sore hands rubbed raw

Helpless

And I'm often stuck to wonder-
Why the fuck we even try-
And the ship keeps going under-
Water flooding from all sides-
And I'm living for the moment-
At least that's what I say-
But the wreck keeps sinking deeper-
Buried thick beneath the clay.

The Flight

I just keep going on
Like the world after heavy rains
Like my alarm after it's seventh snooze
Like the one guy who always raises his hand in
class
Like the birds flying south for the winter
With the wavering strength of a butterfly caught
in a windstorm-
I. Just. Keep. Going. On.
Tattered wings a testament-
To the longest days ever to exist.

Deepest Apologies

I am so tired of the sorries

That slip from my tongue

As if they had been owed

Instead of the reflex they are

And the regret they become

Qualifications

How many poems does it take to be considered a
poet?

One or two or twenty?

Do not ask me.

I do not know it.

Discord

Not everything is build with harmony
In mind
In body
Such as the mind within my body
Or the body in my mind.

Always out of tune.

The Decision

It's not what it seems
This precipice of mine.
Although abrupt and endless
It swept in rather sweetly.
Even with the gift of grace
The thought of crossing makes me cold.
This precipice of mine,
I know
Wants to swallow me whole.

The Question

I am not.

It is so easy to say-

What I'm not.

I know-

What I'm not.

I loathe-

What I'm not.

It's so hard to say

What I AM.

I know-

What I am.

But I also don't.

Which makes it worse-

Because what if I'm something I'm not,

And I just don't know it

Yet.

Defiance

A tired rage builds itself
Up quietly
Ivy through the bricks
A new hive in an old hollowed tree
Unopened voicemails in an inbox
Ice freezing over the bluest of lakes

It does not stop.

To Pasture

I took a ladder to Nowhere.
Just climbed my whole life away.
Until stars brushed my heels-
And the weight seemed to lift-
And I floated away-
To the fields.

An Obituary

It was never me.
It was only ever I.
It grew to be too much,
The pressure cracked what was inside.
And I lied.
AndLiedAndLiedAndLied
Said I had "So much time to bide"
I said "Oh, it doesn't matter. I'm just along for
the ride!"

But I'd died.

Twos

Falling through the abyss into-

I don't even know what we're in to-

At least that's what my heart says

As it lies-

in two

A Metaphor

I'm so single I could die.

A Blessed Curse

22

To walk this path

And walk alone

To places

And people

And worlds

Unknown